Magic, Myth, and M...

ZOMBIE

DO YOU BELIEVE?

This series features creatures that excite our minds. They're magical. They're mythical. They're mysterious. They're also not real. They live in our stories. They're brought to life by our imaginations. Facts about these creatures are based on folklore, legends, and beliefs. We have a rich history of believing in the impossible. But these creatures only live in fantasies and dreams. Monsters do not live under our beds. They live in our heads!

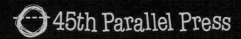
45th Parallel Press

Published in the United States of America by Cherry Lake Publishing
Ann Arbor, Michigan
www.cherrylakepublishing.com

Reading Adviser: Marla Conn MS, Ed., Literacy specialist, Read-Ability, Inc.
Book Design: Felicia Macheske

Photo Credits: © Prezoom.nl/Shutterstock.com, cover, 1; © Lario Tus/Shutterstock.com, 5; © leolintang/ Shutterstock.com, 7; © Esteban Die Ros/Shutterstock.com, 8; © Suzanne Tucker/Shutterstock.com, 11; © Jakub Ridky/Shutterstock.com, 12; © Noska Photo/Shutterstock.com, 15; © Raisa Kanareva/Shutterstock. com, 17; © Ysbrand Cosijn/Shutterstock.com, 18; © Jandrie Lombard/Shutterstock.com, 21; © parinyabinsuk/Shutterstock.com, 22; © Dietmar Temps/Shutterstock.com, 25; © Thanapun/Shutterstock. com, 27; © Thomas Quine/flickr.com/CC BY-SA 2.0, 28

Graphic Elements Throughout: © denniro/Shutterstock.com; © Libellule/Shutterstock.com; © sociologas/ Shutterstock.com; © paprika/Shutterstock.com; © ilolab/Shutterstock.com; © Bruce Rolff/Shutterstock.com

45th Parallel Press is an imprint of Cherry Lake Publishing.

Library of Congress Cataloging-in-Publication Data

Names: Loh-Hagan, Virginia, author.
Title: Zombies : magic, myth, and mystery / by Virginia Loh-Hagan.
Description: Ann Arbor : Cherry Lake Publishing, [2016] | Series: Magic,
 myth, and mystery | Includes bibliographical references and index.
Identifiers: LCCN 2016004927| ISBN 9781634711111 (hardcover) | ISBN
 9781634713092 (pbk.) | ISBN 9781634712101 (pdf) | ISBN 9781634714082 (ebook)
Subjects: LCSH: Zombies–Juvenile literature.
Classification: LCC GR581 .L64 2016 | DDC 398.21–dc23
LC record available at http://lccn.loc.gov/2016004927

Cherry Lake Publishing would like to acknowledge the work of The Partnership for 21st Century Skills.
Please visit www.p21.org for more information.

Printed in the United States of America
Corporate Graphics Inc.

TABLE of CONTENTS

Brain Eaters

What are zombies like? What are some types of zombies?

"Brains. Brains. Must eat brains." Zombies eat brains. They **infect** others. Infect means to spread sickness. They turn humans into zombies. More zombies mean a zombie **apocalypse**. This is when zombies take over. Zombies attack humans.

Zombies are **undead** creatures. Zombies are dead. But they act alive. They don't have free will. They can't think. They lost their former lives. They wear the clothes they died in.

Other undead creatures include mummies, ghosts, and vampires.

Explained by Science!

There are several diseases that cause zombie-like behaviors. A fly bite can cause sleeping sickness. The infection attacks the brain. Victims can't talk. They can't focus. They can't function. They can't move well. They can't sleep. They can become aggressive. Dysarthia affects the part of the brain that controls speech. It's caused by brain damage. Victims can't control their voice muscles. They moan and mumble. They sound like zombies. Necrosis attacks cells. Skin rots off. Victims look like zombies. Their bodies and brains shut down. Yaws is another disease. It infects skin, bones, and joints. It causes painful, oozing sores. Sores occur on faces, legs, arms, and feet. The sores on feet bottoms cause victims to shuffle slowly. Victims walk like zombies.

Zombies have **decomposing** bodies. Their bodies break down. Their skin slowly rots. Their flesh falls off. Their muscles are damaged. They smell really bad.

Zombies limp. They move slowly. They're clumsy. They walk in a zigzag. They hang their heads. They moan. They groan.

Zombies' brains don't work. They're not smart. But they're focused. They destroy. They eat. Nothing stops them.

There's no such thing as a solitary zombie. Where there's one, there's more.

There are different types of zombies. Walkers are the most common. They're regular zombies.

Runner zombies are the most dangerous. They can run. They're fast. They're new zombies. They still have some human strength.

Crawlers don't have legs. Their lower bodies were chopped off. They crawl. They bite ankles.

Spitters spit poison. Their spit burns. It infects. They can spit far.

Bonies are what zombies become. Their flesh has completely rotted off. They have no eyes. They're old zombies.

All types of zombies are dangerous.

Chapter Two

Beware of Zombies!

**How are zombies stronger than humans?
How do zombies eat?**

Zombies are scary. They're dead. But they still move. They bite. They attack. They eat humans.

They're most powerful when first infected. They still have their body parts. They can still move like humans.

They're stronger than humans. They never get tired. They never sleep. They don't feel pain. They live without regular food or water.

They don't need air. They don't breathe. They can live on land. They can live under water. They can't drown.

Zombies aren't hurt by drugs, poisons, gases, electricity, or suffocation.

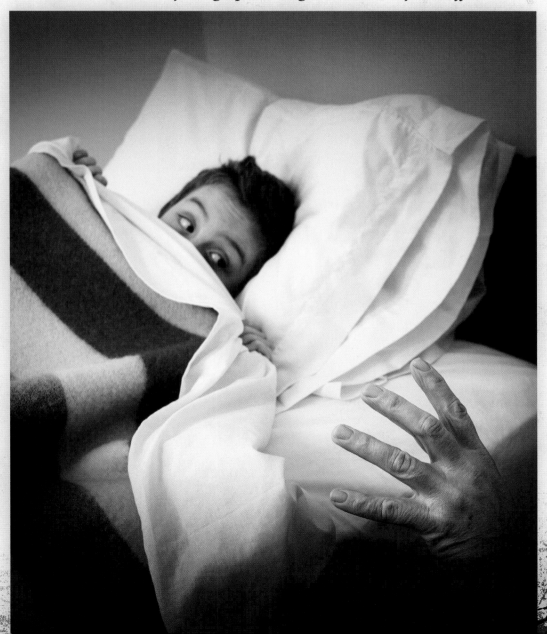

Zombies can hear well. They can smell well. They use these skills to attack.

They like noise. They go to the noise. They attack in **hordes**. Hordes are zombie groups. But zombies don't act like a team. They act separately. They just happen to be doing the same thing.

Their strength is in numbers. They overcome humans. They attack from all sides. They wait for humans to fall. They trap humans. Then they eat. Humans are their food.

Zombies travel in packs.

When Fantasy Meets Reality!

Jewel wasps sting cockroaches. They inject poison. They paralyze the cockroaches' front legs. Paralyze means to not be able to move. Cockroaches can't escape. Jewel wasps sting again. They slide their stingers into the cockroaches' heads. They poke at the brains. They find the right spot. They inject poison. They control the cockroaches' brains. The cockroaches become like zombies. Jewel wasps chew off half the cockroaches' feelers. They drag them to their homes. They lay white eggs on the cockroaches' stomachs. The baby wasps feed on the cockroaches. They chew into the cockroaches' stomachs. They chew on the organs. Then they burst through the cockroaches. That's how jewel wasps are born.

Zombies tend to hang out
where they used to live.

Stronger zombies eat first. They eat brains. They eat organs. They leave the bones. Weaker zombies break open the bones. They eat the stuff inside bones.

Feeding time can be dangerous. Zombies damage each other. They push. They shove. They grab. They pull apart body parts. They don't share food.

Zombies find places with lots of humans. They like hospitals. They like malls. They like churches. These are "hot spots." Zombies prefer cities. They want to be close to food.

Chapter Three

Zombie Weaknesses

What are some ways to kill zombies?
What are some zombie weaknesses?

Most zombies are slower than humans. They can't move well. They're not flexible. They can't use tools. They can't open doors. They can't use stairs. It's easy to kill one zombie. But it's hard to kill a horde.

There are several ways to kill zombies. First, damage their brains. Second, cut off their heads. Third, set them on fire. Fires kill zombies. But zombies won't feel the fires. They'll stumble around. They'll spread the fire.

Fire isn't the best weapon. Swords work better.
Quiet weapons are best. Noise draws more zombies.

Zombies don't have superpowers.
They have fewer abilities than when they were humans.

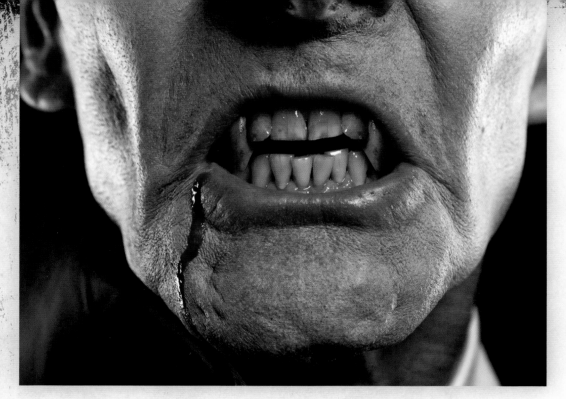

In a fight against vampires, zombies would lose.

Zombies can't see well. They can't see at night. They use other senses.

They can't heal. They can't grow. Sometimes, they lose body parts. Nothing can be done about that.

They don't have many moves. They can't swim. They can't fly. They can only shuffle.

Zombies rot away. They get weaker. They go from walking to crawling. Eventually, they won't move at all.

SURVIVAL TIPS!

- Go to Australia. It's the safest area. Canada is second. The United States is third. These areas were rated based on location, land features, military and weapon access, and population size.

- Feed salt to a zombie. This will make the zombies return to the grave.

- Get fit. Build running skills. Do weight training. Learn martial arts.

- Don't hide in a car unless you have keys. Avoid getting trapped in small spaces.

- Get enough food and water to last 14 to 90 days.

- Stand against a wall. Or stand back-to-back with someone. Make sure no zombies can come behind you.

- Don't use weapons that take time to use. This gives zombies time to bite you.

Chapter Four

Becoming a Zombie

How do people become zombies?

There are several ways to become a zombie. A person dies. Then the person becomes undead. The person becomes a zombie. This process doesn't take long.

A person can get **cursed**. A curse is a magic spell. The curse makes the person undead. These zombies are magical.

A person can get bitten by a zombie. Bites pass

the sickness. The sickness spreads from the zombie to the person.

There is no cure. Once a person is bitten, that person is doomed.

A person can get poisoned. This happens from **radiation**. Energy bursts from a source. The source is usually a bomb. It's also power plant explosions. Radiation attacks anything in its reach.

A person can get a **parasite**. A parasite lives on a **host**. A host can be a person. A common parasite is a worm. The worm attacks the host. It turns a person into a zombie.

Zombie infections can't jump **species**. Species are groups of living things. Humans can't infect animals. Animals can't infect humans.

Dormant infection means that everyone has the potential to be a zombie.

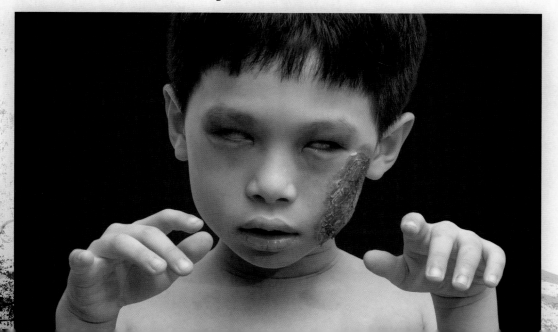

Know the Lingo!

- **Ankle biters:** zombies that don't have legs; also known as crawlers or draggers

- **Chewscrew:** a deep zombie bite that goes into muscle

- **Cluster:** a group of zombies in a small confined area

- **Drone:** the sound a horde makes that can be heard from a distance

- **Grabbers:** zombies trapped inside abandoned cars who reach out of windows to grab victims

- **Grab zone:** the area around a zombie in which a victim can be grabbed

- **Lurkers:** zombies that pretend to be dead; they hide and wait for victims to come close, and then attack

- **Noob:** newly infected zombie

- **RLF:** "reanimated life-form," another word for zombie

- **Swimmers:** bloated and waterlogged zombies, also known as floaters

- **Walkers:** another term for zombies; refers to walking dead

- **ZCORE:** Zombie Coalition Offensive Response Elite, a professional zombie survival group

- **Zombophiles:** fans of zombie films and books

Chapter Five

History of Zombies

How did the word zombie develop? How are zombies featured in different cultures?

Zombie stories started in West Africa. It started with **voodoo**. Voodoo is a religion. It uses folk magic.

Zombie is a special word. It comes from different sources. *Nzambi* is a West African word. It means "spirit of a dead person." It also means "god."

Slaves were brought to America from West Africa. They were sent to Haiti. Haiti is a Caribbean island. Their word for zombie is *jumbie*. It means "ghost."

Slaves also traveled to Louisiana. Their word is

zonbi. This means a person who died and came back.

William Seabrook wrote *The Magic Island*.
He wrote it in 1929. He described his time in Haiti.
He described a dead man coming back to life. He
created the term *zombie*.

Zombies started with the Yoruba tribe in West Africa.

Real-World Connection

There was a zombie-like attack in China. A male bus driver was driving. His name is Dong. A woman driver pulled in front of him. Her name is Du. She blocked his path. He got mad. He jumped on top of her car. He hit the car. She stepped out of her car. She screamed for help. The man jumped on her. He wrestled her to the ground. He bit her face. Du was covered in blood. People tried to pull Dong off her. Police grabbed Dong. Du survived. But she needed surgery to fix her nose and lips. Some believed *jiangshi* took over Dong's body.

Haitians prevent zombies.
They bury bodies under heavy stones.
They watch over the grave for 36 hours.
They cut the heads off.

In Haiti, zombies are created by **bokors**. Bokors are evil priests. They made special drugs. These drugs made people look dead.

Clairvius Narcisse thought he was a zombie slave. He ate the special drugs. He looked dead. He was buried. But he was still alive. He was taken from the grave. He was forced to work on a farm. He worked for several years. Then the owner died. Narcisse returned to his family. People investigated. They found out Narcisse's brother drugged him and sold him to the farm owner. They were fighting over land. His brother wanted to get rid of him.

There are zombies in Chinese stories. Chinese zombies are called *jiangshi*. That means "hopping **corpse**." Corpse is a dead body. They died far from home. They can't rest in peace. They want to get back home. They take energy from humans.

There are zombies in Scandinavian stories. They're called *draugr*. They were fighters. They died. They came back to life. They attack humans.

Long ago, some people were buried alive. Doctors thought they were dead. But they weren't. Thieves dug up their graves. They wanted to steal jewelry. But they got a surprise. The people in the graves were still alive! The thieves thought the dead had risen. These stories made zombies a part of our culture.

Zombie stories have been found in Europe, Asia, North America, Africa, and the Middle East.

Did You Know?

- October 8 is World Zombie Day. Many cities celebrate. People dress as zombies. They walk in a parade.

- Mummies are undead. But they're not zombies. Zombies are always decaying. Mummies are preserved. They're saved from decaying as quickly.

- The Centers for Disease Control and Prevention (CDC) wants people to be prepared. It wants people to survive disasters. It created a plan for zombies. It said, "If zombies did start roaming the streets, CDC would conduct an investigation much like any other disease outbreak."

- George Washington was almost the first "zombie president" of the United States. He died in 1799. His dead body was on ice for three days. William Thornton wanted to bring Washington back to life. He wanted to pump air into Washington's lungs. He wanted to give Washington lamb's blood. Washington's family said no.

- Zombies last longest in cold weather. The cold and snow preserve their bodies.

- There's a zombie law in Haiti. It's a crime to turn people into zombies.

- The 1932 film *White Zombie* was the first appearance of a zombie.

- Zombies are mentioned in *Epic of Gilgamesh*. This story is over 5,000 years old. It features an angry goddess. The goddess threatens to bring the dead back to eat the living.

Consider This!

Take a Position: Read about other undead creatures. (45th Parallel Press has a book about vampires.) Where do you rank zombies in regard to other undead creatures? Which undead creature is the scariest? Argue your point with reasons and evidence.

Say What? What would you do in a zombie apocalypse? Explain your fears. Explain your survival strategies.

Think About It! Dr. Frankenstein's monster is famous. It's made up of dead bodies. It was brought back to life. But is it a zombie? Many zombie fans don't think so. Learn more about Frankenstein's monster. (The book was written by Mary Wollstonecraft Shelley.) Then, decide for yourself.

Learn More

- Hamilton, S. L. *Zombies*. Edina, MN: ABDO Publishing, 2011.
- Jenson-Elliot, Cindy. *Zombies*. San Diego: KidHaven Press, 2006.
- Owen, Ruth. *Zombies and Other Walking Dead*. New York: Bearport Publishing, 2013.

Glossary

apocalypse (uh-POK-uh-lips) the final destruction of the civilized world

bokors (BO-kurz) evil priests in Haiti

corpse (KORPS) a dead body

cursed (KURSD) put under a magical spell

decomposing (dee-kuhm-POHZ-ing) decaying or rotting in the process of dying

hordes (HORDZ) groups of zombies

host (HOHST) a person or the thing providing life to a parasite

infect (in-FEKT) to contaminate, to spread sickness

parasite (PAR-uh-site) a thing living off of a host

radiation (ray-dee-AY-shuhn) energy bursting from a source and spreading poison

species (SPEE-sheez) groups of living things

undead (un-DED) dead but brought back to life

voodoo (VOO-doo) a religion that started in West Africa

Index

About the Author

Dr. Virginia Loh-Hagan is an author, university professor, former classroom teacher, and curriculum designer. She feels like a zombie every morning. She's a big fan of *The Walking Dead*. She lives in San Diego with her very tall husband and very naughty dogs. To learn more about her, visit www.virginialoh.com.